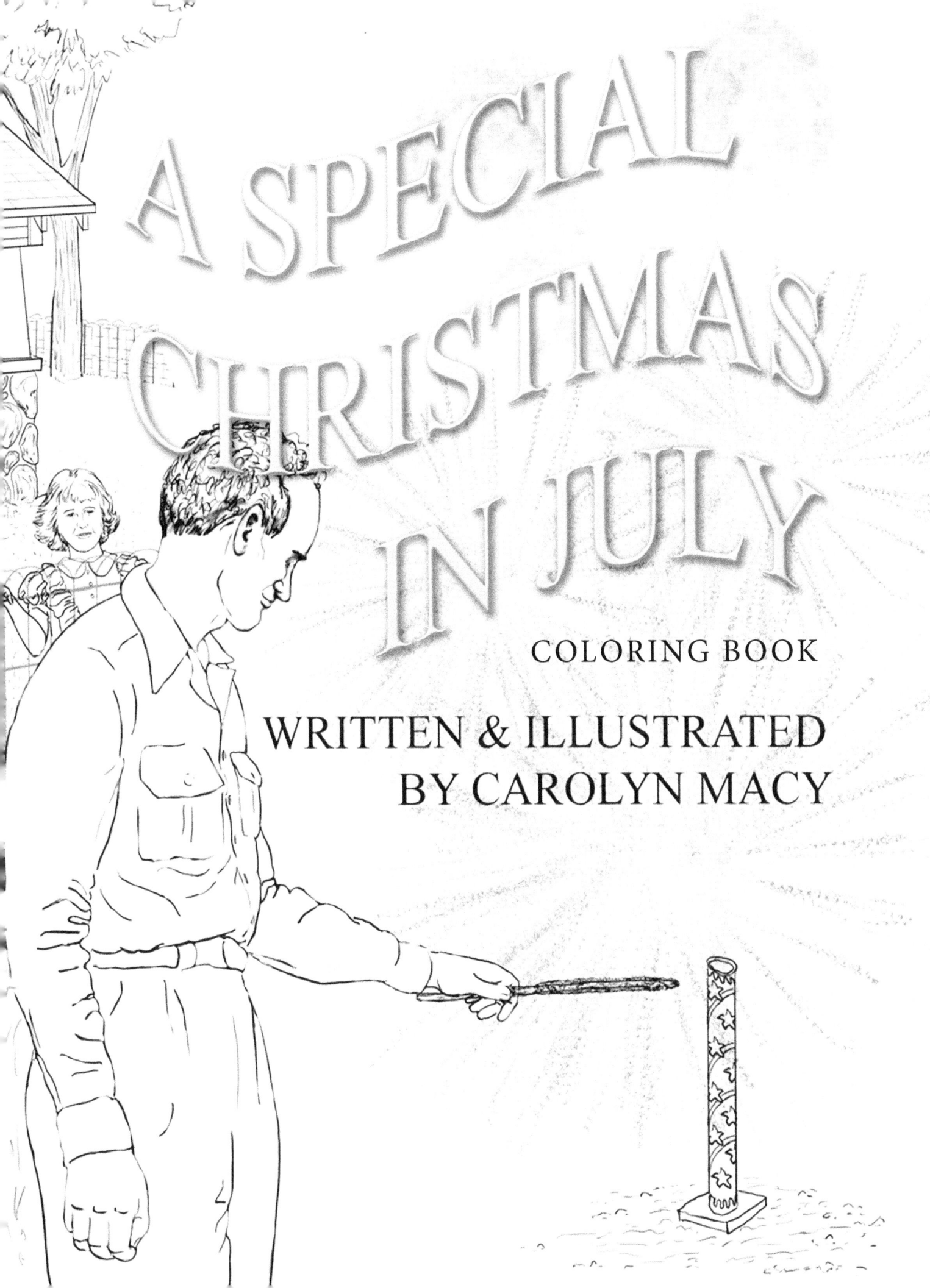

A SPECIAL CHRISTMAS IN JULY

COLORING BOOK

WRITTEN & ILLUSTRATED
BY CAROLYN MACY

Dedicated to my family and friends, particularly to my sisters, Margaret and Francie, and my cousin, David, for their help in memories and pictures.

A Special Christmas in July – Coloring Book
Copyright © 2017 by Carolyn Macy. All rights reserved.

No part of this publication may be reproduced, stored in a retrieval system or transmitted in any way by any means, electronic, mechanical, photocopy, recording or otherwise without the prior permission of the author except as provided by USA copyright law.

Published by Carolyn Macy
6227 81st Avenue N.E. | Norman, Oklahoma 73026 USA
405.401.2012

Book design copyright © 2017 by Carolyn Macy.
Written and Illustrated by Carolyn Macy

Published in the United States of America
ISBN: 978-0-9989127-5-2
JUVENILE NONFICTION / Biography & Autobiography

Today a letter came
 From Uncle Clyde which read,
 "Next week we'll bring the boys
 To spend the month ahead."

We counted down the days
　When cousins would appear
To stay at Grandma's house
　And visit us this year!

Our cousins showing up
   Made summer much more fun
Of finding ways to play
   From dawn to setting sun.

The creek with shallow pools
    Attracted us to wade,
And all along its banks
    We freely roamed and played.

Within our grove of trees,
We built a place to play,
But found it leaked a lot
One very rainy day.

When moonlight filled the sky
And stars above popped out,
We watched the wonders there
With night sounds all about.

By living where we did,

We sometimes had to face

Us stopping play to help
With work around our place.

Each day became so full,

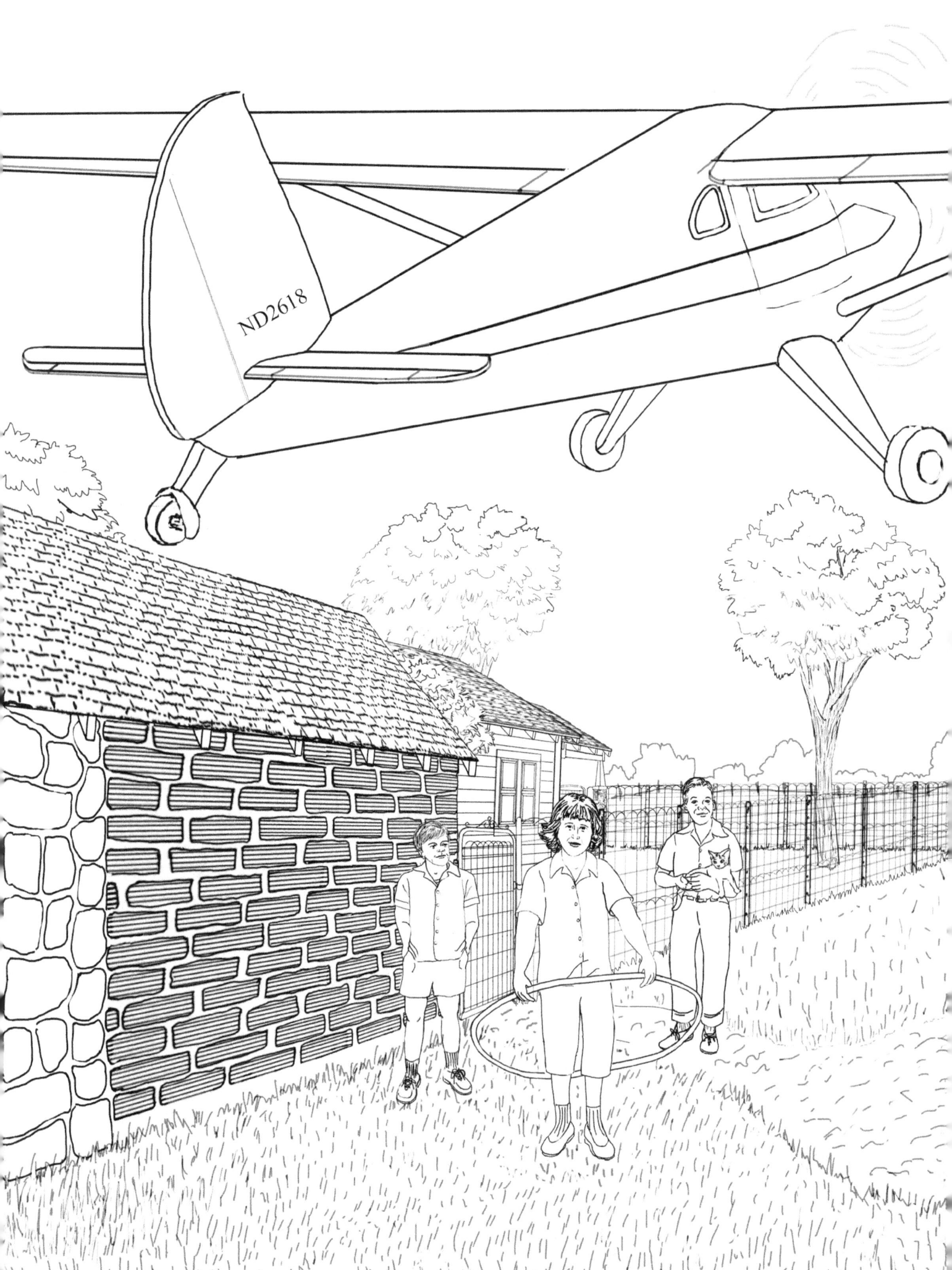

But then one day a sound
   That came from overhead
Caused all of us to stop
   And look above instead.

So loud and low it zoomed
Not far above the ground.
With open-mouths we watched
It circle back around.

Its wings tipped up and down
To send a big "Hello!"
Again it circled back
And flew down very low.

When hearing skyward sounds,
 Our folks all came outside
To see if what they heard
 Might be our Uncle Clyde.

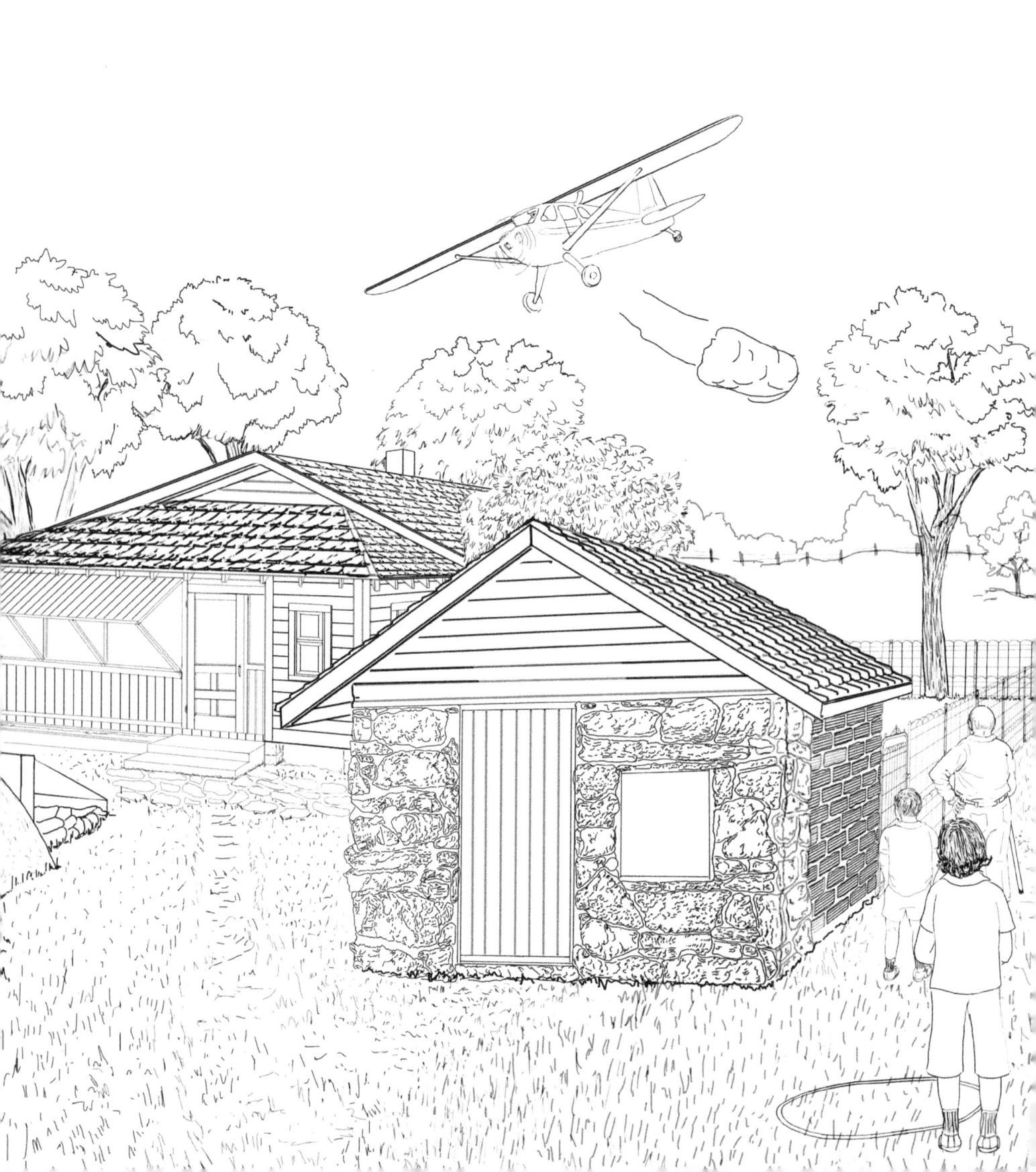

As we kept watching him,
 His plane dipped low again
So he could drop a bag
 Of treasures packed within.

We waved as he once more
Flew over where we stood.

He tipped his wings to us,
Then flew away for good.

We opened up the bag,
 Delivered through the air,

To see what treats it held
For all of us to share.

Delighted with his gifts,
We made a quick reply
To thank our Uncle Clyde
For 'Christmas in July'!

www.ingramcontent.com/pod-product-compliance
Lightning Source LLC
Chambersburg PA
CBHW080416300426
44113CB00015B/2539